PAULE & JEAN-CLAUDE ROUSSEL

THE ART OF FURNITURE
DECORATION

ANDRE DEUTSCH
ULISSEDITIONS

First published in Great Britain in 1995 by
André Deutsch Limited
106 Great Russell Street, London WC1B 3LJ

Copyright © Ulisse Editions 1995
15 rue de Prony, 92600 Asnières – France

General Editor: John Tittensor
Photos: Peter Maidment
Layout: Mario Giamar
Photocomposition: Comp2, Turin
Editing by In-folio, Turin

ISBN 0-233-98951-X

Printed in Hong Kong by Colorcraft

Contents

*At the gateway of the authors' home
in the South of France.*

Preface

It seems more than probable that the first painted wooden object was a prehistoric sculpture, most likely in the shape of an animal or a human being. The 'paint' might have been no more than a touch of mud, added by the sculptor to make his work more realistic. Men were not slow to realize that objects made of wood asked to be painted; and that wood absorbed and gave permanence to the colours they mixed from earth. The results were not always what one might have hoped, but this painting of everyday objects and furniture is as old as mankind itself. In this respect we owe a considerable debt to the ancient Egyptians, whose burial customs, with the help of an extremely dry climate, have bequeathed us superb examples of motifs painted on wood. Their tombs were filled with painted objects, of which the sarcophagus was often the centrepiece. The tomb of Meket-Re at Thebes (around 2000 BC) and that of Tutenkhamen (1338 BC) are particularly striking in this regard.

Italy and Greece, countries that did not possess the same climatic advantages, have unfortunately left us fewer examples. We know, however, that the Greeks actually went as far as to paint stone, notably statues and temples. In the frescoes of Pompeii we note the presence of painted objects and pieces of furniture: in the diningroom of the imperial villa, a mural shows a painted bed. The legacy of the Middle Ages is not very extensive: we find only a few wooden chests in certain castles, and polychrome wooden statues in churches.

Our native France is not particularly rich in painted furniture, and the examples that we find here are limited to certain definite localities. The wood-painting tradition was particularly vigorous in Alsace, where it was influenced by the work of German artists. The Alsace Museum in Strasbourg has some fine examples on show. In the South of France, the town of Uzès was, in the 18th and 19th centuries, the source of painted wardrobes that are now much coveted – and extremely rare. Two of these wardrobes are on show in the Regional Art Museum in Nimes, but most of the others are in private hands. The only really widespread everyday object in painted wood was the grandfather clock so prized by the peasantry; in the 19th century just about every

family owned one. These clocks were as a general rule painted with a false 'woodgrain' effect, then decorated with linework, ears of corn and so on.

In the countries of Central Europe we discovered an incredibly rich store of peasant art – a discovery that filled us with admiration and triggered the love of painted wood that motivates our work today. In Austria, Germany, Switzerland, Rumania, Hungary, Slovakia and the Czech Republic the examples are innumerable.

As far as those in museums are concerned, no admirer of painted furniture should miss visiting the collections of the Tirolervolkskunstmuseum in Innsbruck, and the Munchen Bayerisches Landemuseum in Munich. The north of Europe was just as prolific: Poland, Norway, Sweden, Denmark and other countries all have their own tradition. The art of furniture painting in Europe reached its high point in the 18th and 19th centuries, but in the 20th century a decline set in. Our aim was to maintain the tradition, but to treat it as a living art – and this meant that we had to take a personal, creative approach.

For twenty years now, in a tiny village in the South of France, we've been working with the same undiminished pleasure; and the sign that hangs in front of our workshop – 'Rondeur des jours' – describes in French our passion for our work, and the feeling of fullness, freedom and spontaneity our craft brings us. We both have a degree in art history and Paule is a trained painter as well – but as far as our techniques of painting on wood are concerned, we had to teach ourselves everything from scratch. In this book, we'd like to share the fruits of our years of experience with you.

Jean-Claude is the one who looks after the preparatory side of things – stripping back the wood, restoration and base-coats – as well as the finishing stages when the varnish or the patina is applied. Paule designs and executes all the painted motifs.

We haven't written this book as an exercise in nostalgia or to speak of weird and wonderful things.

We're not going to send you off, either, into exotic lands in search of wondrous substances.

We're simply going to talk about our way of working, and there's nothing at all complicated about it: the materials you'll need are all modern products that you'll find on sale everywhere.

1. *Painting on Wood*

Surfaces and precautionary measures

What sort of thing can you paint?

Just about any object made of wood: tubs, boxes, chests, lampstands, old furniture you've bought in an antique shop, new furniture in raw wood. And don't neglect the possibilities of door-frames, panelling, wainscoting and so on.

What wood should you use?

Any wood that does not have a pronounced colour will do: pine, fir, beech, etc.

A word of warning

In certain cases the knots in pine and fir wood lead to staining. It's a good idea to cover them with a coat of matt varnish before you start. Some woods also contain pockets of resin which can rise to the surface even when the painting is finished. To avoid this problem, burn them out with a hot iron – a soldering iron, for example – then plug the hole with wood-filler. We advise against using high-tannin woods such as oak and walnut; they too can produce brown stains and the special varnish needed to prevent this makes the work more difficult and the end result more fragile.

Other surfaces

Certain 'reconstituted' woods – plywood for example – are agreable to work on and give good results. In addition, they don't split with the passing of time, which is always a risk with solid pieces of wood.

The basic equipment for stripping wood before painting.

A bedside table waiting to be stripped back.

Preparing the surfaces

For a good, durable result, your wood has to be absolutely clean before you start painting. So if the object in question is already painted, it will need careful stripping-back. There are several ways of going about this.

The caustic soda method

What's good about this method of stripping wood is that it's simple, cheap and works well in about 80% of cases. Ideally, stripping back is done out of doors, using, among other things, a garden hose. A word of warning here: as the mixture we're going to suggest can produce severe burns, you'll need to protect your hands with a tough pair of gloves and make sure you don't splash the mix around. The 'recipe' we use is as follows:

Stripper recipe
– Take a standard-size plastic bucket.
– Fill the bucket to the three-quarter mark with hot water.
– Add a can of caustic soda.
– Get the mixture moving by stirring, then gradually pour in a third of a packet of ordinary wallpaper glue.

And now to work!
– With a paper-hanger's brush on a long handle, cover the painted areas with stripping mixture.
– Wait twenty minutes for the mixture to take effect.
– Rinse down well with a high-pressure garden hose.
– Repeat the operation as often as necessary.
– Let the article in question dry for 10 days, in a cool place and out of the sun.
Sometimes this method leads to a blackening of the wood, in which case you'll have to bleach it while it's still wet, using hydrogen peroxide.

Heat stripping

If the paint turns out to be highly resistant, use a heat-stripper: either an electric model or one that runs off a bottle of gas. Both types are easy to find in hardware stores and do-it-yourself shops. All you have to do is direct a jet of hot air from the stripper on to the paint; the heat will soften the paint and then you can scrape it off with

Application of the home-made stripping mixture.

A good wash-down with a hose gets rid of the stripping mixture and the paint.

a metal spatula. It's a good idea, if you use the heat method, to finish the job with an application of the caustic soda mixture.

Bath stripping

In certain extreme cases you will have no choice but to seek out the services of a professional who will strip your item in a caustic soda bath. This method is totally effective, but sometimes the æsthetic price is high: the surface of the wood turns disagreeably furry and the joints loosen up. Think twice before you take the plunge.

Restoration: all you need for filling and sanding back.

Stripping varnished or waxed wood

In these two cases you can opt for decidedly gentler solutions:

– for waxed surfaces, a good all-purpose kitchen cleanser;

– for varnish, acetone or a product with similar properties.

Restoring damaged surfaces

Once you've got your wood perfectly clean and dry, a certain amount of restoration will probably be necessary before you can get down to painting it.

Holes and cracks

Small holes and cracks can be filled with spackle or some other filler. Once the spackle has dried, rub it back well with sandpaper and wire wool.

Moving parts

In the case of furniture, make sure before you start that the drawers, doors, locks, etc. are in good working order. Don't forget, either, that the thickness of a coat of paint can cause sticking; you may have to plane some surfaces back a little.

What equipment do you need?

Paint

We use – and heartily recommend – the ordinary vinyl or acrylic matt paints you find in any paint shop or do-it-yourself centre.

They are all waterbased, which means they're extremely easy to work with: you can apply them with no difficulty whatsoever to just about any surface, they dry quickly, they give a good tough finish and their colours don't fade over time. And we ought to know: we've been using the same ones, more or less, for twenty years now.

Paints and varnishes: Our way of working doesn't call for exotic products.

Right: Creating a patina is a very simple matter.

As a rule any well-known brand will do the job, but we've found that it's best not to mix your brands. The slightest incompatibility can have a disastrous effect on the durability of the final result. As far as colours go, the range is virtually unlimited. Naturally the choice is up to you, but we advise you to start off with a selection of darker-toned paints; you can then lighten them at will just by adding white.If you want to create faded, slightly 'aged' effects, you'll need some black as well. This is because the basic colours available in the shops are always very strong – you'll be surprised sometimes at the amount of black you need to get the look you're after. When you embark on a project you should have all the paint you're going to need ready in plastic or glass pots – we get through a lot of little yoghurt containers this way. Make sure there's an adequate amount

of paint at the outset; that way you'll always have exactly the same colour as the work goes ahead. We advise against using an artist's palette, as the quantity often turns out to be insufficient.

Varnishes

Although they're totally insoluble once they've dried, acrylic and vinyl paints need a coat of varnish to give a tough, lasting finish. This also gives you the chance to choose exactly the final look you want. We've started using the new water-based varnishes, which are very agreable to work with: they're fast-drying, you can wash your brushes out in water, those unpleasant smells are gone and there's no problem with yellowing over time.

Patinas

Creating a patina involves tarnishing the paint in such a way as to 'age' it artificially. To get this effect we use a mixture of Judean bitumen diluted with turpentine or white spirit. To save yourself time and effort, you can try the various ready-to-use patinas available in the shops.

*With just a few different kinds
of brush, you can create all the decors
and motifs mentioned in this book.*

Walnut stain
This is a blackish powder which
dissolves in water and allows
you to deepen the colour of the
wood you're working with.

Brushes
We're a long way from the world
of watercolours and painting
in oils here. Frankly, it just isn't
worth the trouble of spending

a lot of money on high-quality
brushes. No brush lasts long
when you're using vinyl paints
and you can get by perfectly well
if you equip yourself with the
following range:

– *For the backgrounds* Plain
ordinary paintbrushes – choose
your sizes according to the
surfaces you have to cover.

– *For the motifs* The choice
is up to you, but we use
fine-pointed artists' brushes
of various sizes (from n° 2 up
to n° 10) and the round-ended
brushes schoolchildren use –
these are very cheap indeed.

– *For stippled effects* There's
nothing better than those small,
flat, stiff brushes you find

11

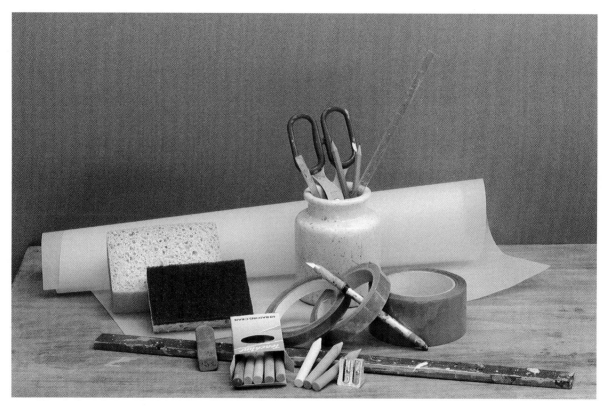

Odds and ends: a few 'extras' that come in handy.

on sale – cheap – just about everywhere.

Other equipment
– Pencils: the pencils should be neither too hard nor too soft – in other words the good old HB will do the job in most situations.

– School chalk: white for use on coloured backgrounds, coloured for use on white backgrounds.

– A good long ruler.

– Tracing paper.

– Pencil sharpener, eraser, scissors, craft knife.

– Masking tape.

– Sandpaper.

– Sponges.

– Scotchbrite pads.

– Pieces of cloth.

Preparing your backgrounds

What kind of background?

The three techniques we use are as follows:

– Painting the background directly on to the raw wood.

– Painting the background on to a base-coat – white, beige or another colour.

– 'Sponging'.

Painting the background directly on to raw wood

(See page 58). This approach is the least complicated, but can only be used when the wood is in good condition and well stripped-back. You get the best results on wood that's been at least lightly tinted, as the wearing-back of the paint will
let the surface of the wood show through in places. The application of the background takes place in five stages:

1. With a flat paintbrush, cover the surface with a walnut stain mixture – the concentration is up to you. Let dry for 12 hours.

2. Paint the entire surface with a matt acrylic varnish. Let dry for 12 hours.

3. Rub down with fine sandpaper, taking care to follow the grain of the wood at all times.

4. Using a normal paintbrush, cover the surface with a uniform coat of the colour of your choice. Make sure your brushstrokes are even and well-directed. Let dry for 12 hours.

5. Using a scotchbrite soaked in water, rub back the final coat of paint so as to let the wood show through in places. Don't rub too hard at first – but don't forget, either, that the various edges, angles, mouldings, etc. will need a bit more pressure to get the right effect.

Painting the background on to a beige base-coat

(See page 64) This is one of our most frequent ways of working – but you don't have to use beige if you don't want to. Your choice of colour will depend on the nature of the project you have in mind and the effects you want to achieve. If the surface of the wood shows numerous flaws, you're better off applying a base-coat before proceeding to the application of the final colour. The following ways of working will enable you to establish a good even background and to cover up such flaws as stains or filled-in areas.

1. Using an ordinary paintbrush, cover the surface with a coat of beige paint. This can be as dark or light as you like, but it should be fairly close to the colour of the wood. Let dry for 12 hours.

2. Rub back with fine sandpaper, taking care to follow the grain of the wood.

3. Add a second coat of paint, of the same colour as the first. Let dry for 12 hours.

4. Rub back once more with fine sandpaper.

5. Using a standard paintbrush, cover the whole surface with a single coat of the colour you've chosen for the background. Let dry for 12 hours.

6. Using a scotchbrite soaked in water, rub back the final coat of paint so as to let the beige base-coat show through in places. Don't rub too hard at first – but don't forget that here too the various edges, angles, mouldings, etc. will need extra pressure to get the right look.

Painting the background on to a white base-coat

The procedure is exactly the same as for the beige base-coat, but the final rubbing-back with the scotchbrite creates a different visual effect.

'Sponging'

(See page 71) The application of a white base-coat allows you to obtain a range of pleasing 'wiped' effects. To do this, follow the procedure outlined below:

1. Using a paintbrush, apply two even coats of white vinyl paint to the surface, allowing a drying time of 12 hours between coats. Rub each coat back with fine sandpaper once it is dry.

2. Take the colour of your choice and dilute it, to make it more liquid and free-flowing.

3. Apply the diluted paint in a fairly 'approximate' way with a paintbrush. Work in stages: first one side of the piece of furniture, then the top.

4. Take a moist (but not soaking wet) rectangular sponge, and smooth it over the wet paint, following the grain of the wood at all times.

5. Let dry for 12 hours.

6. Rub the different surfaces back lightly with a wet scotchbrite, using extra pressure on the edges, angles and so on. Working this way is an excellent means of accentuating the 'veining' of the wood.

Decoration

So you've finished your background – and already you have the impression of a completely different piece of furniture. It looks brand new, or as if it had shed its old skin. But you haven't finished yet. You're going to add decorative mouldings, linework, panels and motifs which will complete the metamorphosis of the piece you began with.

Mouldings

(See page 58) Once the background colour is in place, you can set about putting the accent on the 'architecture' of the piece of furniture, by using another colour on different parts of it:

– on the mouldings that surround the panels;

– on the protruding edge of the top of the piece;

– on the cornices;

– on other details that stand out more or less from the surface.

This work is best done with a n° 16 or n° 18 pointed brush. When you're following a raised surface, it's usually quite easy to work freehand.

Panels

And what happens when you're faced with a completely flat surface – no mouldings, nothing? Well, why not give it some extra life by adding false panels?

Or maybe the piece of furniture contains a panel that seems to you to be too big?

You can 'cut it down to size' by creating a smaller panel inside it. In both cases you have two possibilities:

Linework

First off, draw the line with your HB pencil and a ruler. Then, if you've got a sufficiently sure hand, follow this guideline freehand, using a little n° 4 or n° 6 pointed brush. But then, not everybody has the gift of being able to paint freehand in which case, define your line clearly with a strip of scotch tape running down each side, then just paint the area in between.

Bands of a different colour

(See page 71) Begin as for the lines described immediately above, drawing the shape of the panel with an HB pencil and – don't forget – a ruler. Then follow this guideline, using transparent scotch tape to mark out the areas to be painted.

14

Drawing

We use two techniques:

Tracing

(See page 58) This is the method that beginners feel most at home with, because the tracing technique allows you to create a symmetrical design without too much trouble.

Here's how you go about it:

1. Take a piece of tracing paper the size of the panel you're going to work on.

2. Fold the tracing paper very precisely in four. This will give you vertical and horizontal midlines which will be very useful in the preparation of your motif. Unfold the sheet.

3. The drawing should be done using a normal HB pencil.

4. If the motif you have in mind is symmetrical, you'll only need to draw one half of it. Later, by folding the paper in two, you'll be able to transfer the design on to the other half of the panel without any difficulty.

This design can of course be used more than once – if your piece has two doors or two identical panels, for example. With a bit of luck you might even be able to use it for another piece altogether.

Chalk

(See page 35) If it's a question of creating a single motif, you can do this by drawing directly with the chalk: using white chalk on coloured backgrounds and coloured chalk on white backgrounds. Using chalk is simple and there's the added advantage of being able to rub out your mistakes easily. Don't forget that the centring of your designs is a major consideration; this means you need to put your midlines in place before you start.

Painting a motif

This technique will be explained in Chapter 2, according to the different kinds of motifs presented. Once your design has dried, you can soften it down, if you want to, by rubbing it lightly with fine sandpaper.

Varnishing

To get a really durable final finish on any piece of furniture we've decorated, we apply three coats of varnish. Between each coat we allow the full drying time suggested by the manufacturer. Varnishing makes the piece washable and also means you can add a patina, without risk of staining or other undesirable after-effects.

The patina

If you make up your own patina from Judean bitumen bought in powder form, you'll need to prepare your mixture several days in advance; this gives the powder the time it needs to dissolve properly in the turpentine.

The recipe

Pour 25 cl of turpentine into a 50 cl glass container, add 4 soup spoons of bitumen powder and mix well. The result is a dark, syrupy substance which can be made as light as you like by adding more turpêntine.

Application

1. Brush the mixture onto the surface, with a brush you're not going to use for anything else.

2. Wipe off the superfluous patina with a cotton cloth. According to how vigorously and how often you wipe the surface down, you'll get a light, medium or dark brown film.

3. Let dry.

4. Lightly moisten a cloth with white spirit, then rub the surfaces of the piece of furniture. By doing this you'll bring out the veining of the wood and the highlights of the

motifs; at the same time this will have the effect of making the shadowed areas – in the corners and the grooves – look darker, as if the paint has aged.

N.B. The beginner needs to understand that the application of a patina is quite a delicate operation and calls for a touch that only comes with experience. The important thing is not to let yourself get discouraged if the initial results are unsatisfactory; all you have to do is wipe the surface clean with a cloth soaked in white spirit – then start again. The patina will take about two weeks to dry completely. The surface it provides will resist moisture quite well, but can be easily damaged by greasy substances.

One thing you must absolutely not do is apply wax or wax-based polish to the patina. To 'fix' it – this is especially necessary on such surfaces as table-tops – you can add a light coat of varnish. This is done by quickly brushing on an acrylic varnish diluted with water, then immediately wiping over the surface with kitchen-paper. This leaves a protective film of varnish on the patina.

2. Examples of Painted Motifs

Flowers

Flowers – and epecially roses – are the most frequently used of all the traditional motifs. Some of them are not presented in a particularly realistic manner, but in this type of decoration you have the right to let your imagination go a little.

The colours used are indicated on the palette (page 18).

You'll also need white, which is used for all the motifs.

An arrow signals that white has been used to lighten a given colour.

The backgrounds have all been painted with green C, as marked on the palette.

As far as the painting of the actual flowers goes, you generally begin with the leaves. For the leaves with pointed ends, use a small pointed brush; for the rounded leaves you'll need a round-tipped brush.

The leaves

The technique consists in spreading a mid-green which overlaps the drawn outline a little, then adding a touch of white on one of the edges to create a highlight. The white part should be blurred quickly, while the colours are still wet; for this you can use the same brush as for the mid-green.

You can now do the same thing on the other side of the leaf, but using instead a touch of a darker green: the aim being to give some depth to the leaf as a whole. Finish up with the veins of the leaves, using a very fine pointed brush. We advise you to work only on one leaf at a time, as the paint dries quickly. When you've finished a particular part of a motif, you can speed the drying up with a hairdryer.

This also has the advantage of avoiding the smudging that occurs if your painting hand contacts wet paint.

FLOWERS

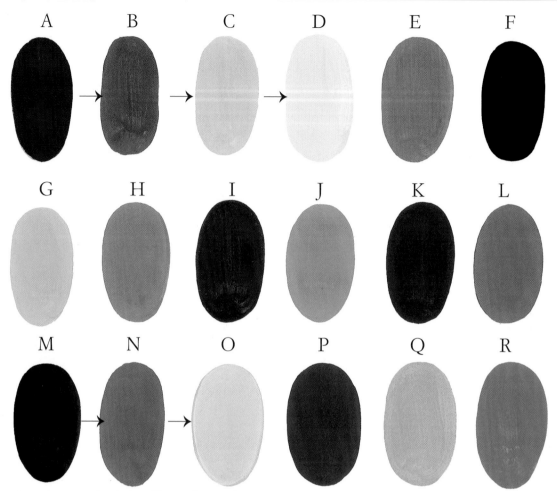

A   B   C   D   E   F

G   H   I   J   K   L

M   N   O   P   Q   R

The palette. An arrow signals the addition of some white.

example 1

1   2   3   4

Rose

Colours
Leaves A
Flower M
Spots J

1. Spread the dark red – two layers are often necessary.
2. Place a white line along the edge of the petals, then soften it with the brush used for the red. Draw a white circle fairly close to the edge, then blur it towards the inside. The petals are always painted with quick touches of the brush while the colours are still wet. Finish with the yellow dots in the heart of the flower.

example 2

Rose

Colours
Leaves D
Flower H
Heart I,F

A little black adds depth to the heart of the rose.

example 3

Rose

Colours
Leaves E
Flower N
Heart M

4. Begin with the big petal and finish on the inside.

example 4

Rose

Colours
Leaves B, A
Flower O
Heart N

Each petal is shaped with a stroke of a round-tipped brush.

example 5

Rose

Colours
Leaves A
Flower J
Heart K

The flowers are not drawn; each one is shaped with a stroke of a round-tipped brush.

example 6

Wild rose

Colours
Leaves D, B
Flower O
Heart N

2. Soften the white.
3. Soften the rose (N).
4. Finish with the heart and the dots.

example 7

Round petals

Colours
Leaves B
Flower N
Heart M

3. Soften the white.
4. Finish in this order: the heart, the white highlights and the dots.

example 8

Tulip

Colours
Leaves B, A
Flower J
Heart I

2. Soften the shadow (I)
3. A brushstroke going from the top downwards.

example 9

Carnation

Colours
Leaves A
Flower M

2. Here you have to start with the flower.
3. Work from the top down, with a pointed brush.
4. Paint 3 rows of petals, then finish with the calyx.

example 10

Daisy

Colours
Leaves B
Flower J

1. The outline of the flower is very light, so as not to show through the paint.
3. Each petal is a stroke of a round-tipped brush. Work from the outside in.
4. Add in a round yellow centre, then 2 white highlights.

example 11

Zinnia

Colours
Leaves B, A
Flower L
Heart M

3. Soften the first row of petals.
4. Finish with the centre and add the dots last.

example 12

Lily of the Valley

Colours
Leaves B, A
Flower G
Shadow H

This is a pretty little motif which can be used in compositions with larger flowers: roses for example.

example 13

Convolvulus

Colours
Leaves B, A
Flower R
Lines Q, R
Heart J

Start with the flower.
2. Soften the white heart by dabbing lightly with a small brush.
3. Paint the front petal, then put in the mauve lines with a pointed brush.

example 14

Pansy

Colours
Leaves D
Flowers Q
Heart J

This was a very popular turn-of-the-century motif.

example 15

Blueberry

Colours
Leaves B, A
Flowers R
Heart R, Q

2. Each leaf is a single stroke with a round-tipped brush.
3. For each petal: 3 strokes of a pointed brush.

example 16

Star anemone

Colours
Leaves A
Flower O
Heart and
   veins P

3. Soften the rose (P) by dabbing with a small flat brush.
4. Paint the white heart, the veins, then the dots.

example 17

Lesser celandine

Colours
Leaves A
Flowers K

3. Charge your brush with white, then use a circular stroke.

example 18

Clover

Colours
Leaves B, A
Flower P

3. Working from the top down, use little strokes of a round-tipped brush dipped in white.

FRUITS

As for the flowers, it's best to begin with the leaves, then to paint the actual fruit.

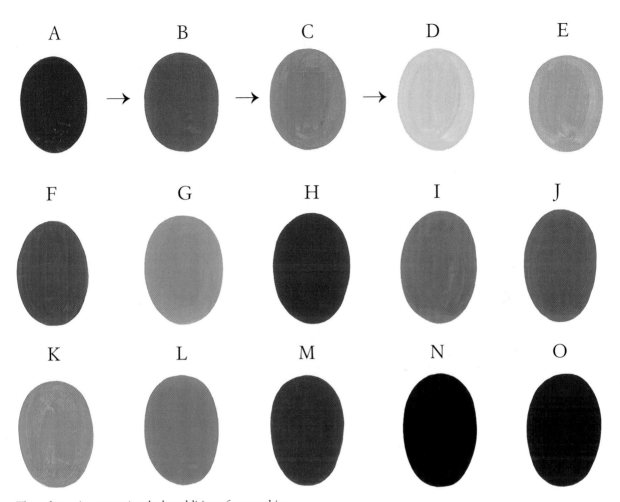

The palette. An arrow signals the addition of some white.

example 1

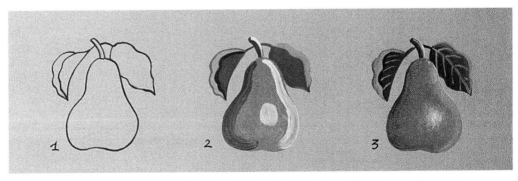

Pear

Colours
Leaves A, B, D
Fruit K
Shading M

2. After painting the background (K), place a white stroke on one side of the pear and a brown stroke on the other. Soften while wet. Finish with the highlight in the middle of the fruit.

example 2

Apple

Colours
Leaves C
Fruit J

2. The procedure is the same as for the pear.

example 3

Lemon

Colours
Leaves A, D
Fruit K
Shadow L

When the lemons are finished, add in the stem.

example 4

Cherry

Colours
Leaves A, C
Fruit O
Shadow N
Stalks M

Finish the two side cherries (shadows and softened highlights), before painting the middle one.

example 5

Bilberry

Colours
Leaves C
Fruit F

The two leaves that partly cover some of the berries should be painted last.

example 6

Strawberry

Colours
Leaves C, A
Fruit O, N

When the shadow and the highlight have been correctly softened (stage 2), add the dark dots, then some little white highlights.

example 7

Peach

Colours
Leaves B, C
Fruit I, K
Shadow H

Firstly, soften the colours K and H, then the white highlights. You can put in the pink of both peaches at the same time if you like, but first you'll need to finish off the shape of the lower one.

example 8

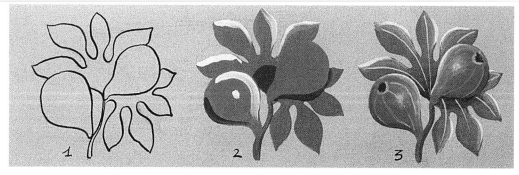

Fig

Colours
Leaves C, B
Fruit G
Shadow H
Stem L, B

The little white veins are added last.

example 9

Pomegranate

Colours
Leaves A, D
Fruit K
Shadow L
Interior N,I

On the inside, once you've placed the dark red, you have to work fast with a little round-tipped brush, adding a lighter pink into the wet paint for the seeds. Finish the seeds with a white highlight.

example 10

Redcurants

Colours
Leaves E, C
Fruit H
Dots N

Use a round-tipped brush for all your round shapes.

example 11

Grapes

Colours
Leaves C
Fruit G
Stem M

While the base-colour is still wet, add in the grapes in white, with a round-tipped brush. Finish with the white highlights: a dot in the centre and a quick brushstroke on the side.

example 12

Raspberries

Colours
Leaves C, B
Fruit H

Firstly, paint the general shape of the fruit, then add in the little bumps before the paint dries. Paint each berry in white, with a round-tipped brush. Adding a white dot at the end will lighten up the berries.

example 13

Acorn

Colours
Leaves E,B
Acorns L, M

Paint the stem and the cups first, then finish with the acorn.

example 14

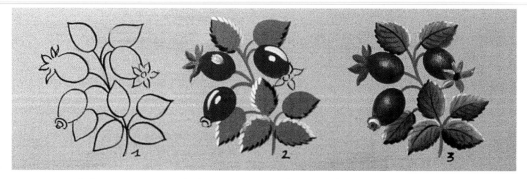

Rosehips

Colours
Leaves C, A
Fruit A, B
Stem M, A

Paint the red body of the fruit first, then the beige sepals.

example 15

Elderberries

Colours
Leaves C, D
Fruit A, B
Stem M, A

For the berries, paint the dark green base-coat first, add a lighter green highlight, then a last little white dot.

example 16

Wheat

Colours
Leaves L
Grains L
Shadow M

Finish with the central row of grains.

example 17

Arbutus berries

Colours
Leaves A, C
Fruit O

Soften the white highlight by dabbing hard. Add little white dots to show the roughness of the skin.

example 18

Olives

Colours
Leaves D, C
Fruit C, B

Once you've softened the shadow and the highlights, put in the dark spot at the base of each olive. Put a white circle around the spot, add in the highlights with a long-headed brush, then a dot. Redefine the stem where it meets the olive.

BASKETS

The palette:

For these two examples you have to work fast, 'wet in wet'.

A. To capture the crisscross effect, all you have to do is accentuate the lit side with pure white and the shadow side with dark brown.

B. Begin with the vertical lines (B3).

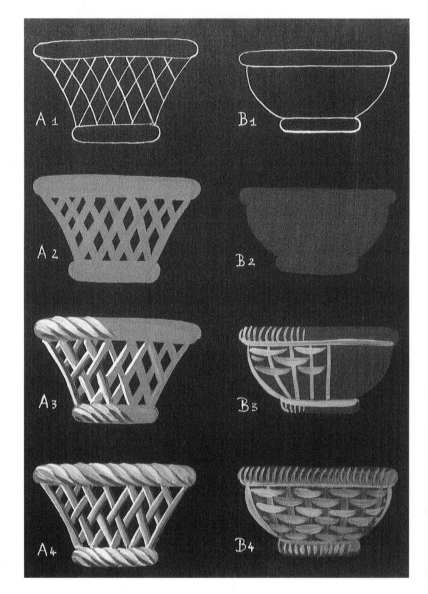

BOWS

A. Indicate the highlights first, then soften them. Finish with the shadows.

B. The central part of the bow is put in last.

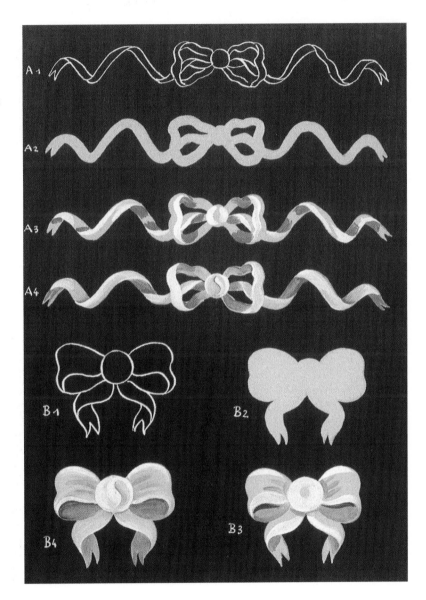

BIRDS

The palette:

A. It would be best to soften the red belly area with beige before adding in the wing. When you've softened the white edge of the wing, you could always suggest the feathers, with quick wet in wet brushstrokes.

B. Proceed in the same way as for A. Paint the body of the bird before the wing.

A CHOICE OF COMPOSITIONS

The palette:

We're going to start this section by showing you a selection of motifs created in our studio, then another group inspired by traditional designs. Unlike the furniture painters of old, we prefer our furniture decorated in a more light and uncluttered way. Covering the entire surface with painted designs doesn't necessarily give the best possible result. In the museums you'll see very elaborate examples of furniture decoration; but don't forget that they can be difficult to execute – and to live with.

Decor: a basket of fruit, painted in several stages (design: Rondeur des Jours).

Referring back to the preceding examples of fruit, we've used grapes (example 11), apples (example 2), pears (example 1), peaches (example 7), raspberries (example 12) and, of course, the basket (page 32).

1. The design is first drawn in white chalk.

Working in stages

1. Draw the design in white chalk.

2. Paint in the leaves at the top.

3. Paint the basket.

4. Paint the grapes.

5. Bring in the raspberries, then the leaves falling over the rim of the basket.

6. Paint in the peaches.

7. For the highlight, add a drop of white and soften it with a small flat brush.

8. Finish with the 3 central pieces of fruit.

9. Let the picture dry thoroughly (12 hours). Then apply three layers of varnish. Here we've opted for a matt finish.

10. Paint on the patina with a broad brush.

11. Wipe off the excess patina with a piece of cloth.

2. Painting in the foliage.

36

3. The basket is painted in.

4. Working on the grapes.

5. When the raspberries are finished, it's the turn of the leaves near the rim of the basket.

6. Right: *Painting the peaches*

7. Below left: *For the highlight, a drop of white is softened down with a small flat brush.*

8. Below right: *We finish with the three central pieces of fruit.*

9. When the picture has dried for
12 hours, you can apply three layers of
varnish. For this particular piece we chose
a matt varnish.

10. *Brushing on the patina.*

11. *Wiping off the excess patina.*

The palette:

COMPOSITION 1
Design: Rondeur des jours.
Bird, elderberries, arbutus
berries, daisies.

The palette:

COMPOSITION 2
Design: Rondeur des jours.
Wheat, olives.

The palette:

COMPOSITION 3
Design: Rondeur des jours.
Small roses, bows.

The palette:

COMPOSITION 4
Inspired by a 19th century
German design.

The palette:

Rondeur des jours

COMPOSITION 5
A 19th century motif from the
Canton de Vaud, in Switzerland.

The palette:

COMPOSITION 6
Inspired by a 19th century
Austrian design.

3. *Painting Everyday Objects and Furniture*

Up until now you've been learning to create painted motifs and bring them together into simple compositions. Now it's time to put what you've learnt into practice, in the context of specific pieces of furniture – a much more demanding situation to be sure, but one that will bring you enormous satisfaction. Before you get into the business of painting a piece of furniture, it would be a good idea to practise on some smaller wooden objects.

A series of wooden tubs

For these tubs we're going to use the technique for painting directly on to wood (see Chapter 1).

Painting step by step

1. Darken the wood first with walnut stain, then leave the tub to dry (12 hours).

2. Paint on a matt acrylic varnish, let dry for 12 hours, then rub back with fine sandpaper.

3. Paint on a good even coat of the colour you've chosen, and let dry for 12 hours.

4. Rub the surface of the paint back with a wet scotchbrite.

The background is in place and now the tubs are ready to be decorated.

A selection of tubs in raw wood.

The palette:

The same tubs in their finished state.

5. Draw your design directly on to the surface with white chalk – a lot easier than trying to use tracing paper on a curved surface.

6. Now paint the motif:
– first the leaves;
– then the fruit.

For the lemons, see the fruit motif pages, example 3. For the other tubs we chose grapes

(example 11), figs (example 8), olives (example 18) and acorns (example 13).

7. When the motif is thoroughly dry, varnish the tubs, using three coats of a satin-finish acrylic varnish.

8. Apply the patina, using the Judean bitumen/turpentine mixture and following the instructions on page 15.

*2. Cover the tub with a matt acrylic
varnish, let dry for 12 hours, and rub
back with fine sandpaper.*

1. Opposite page: *Firstly, darken
the colour of the wood with walnut stain.
Then leave to dry 12 hours.*

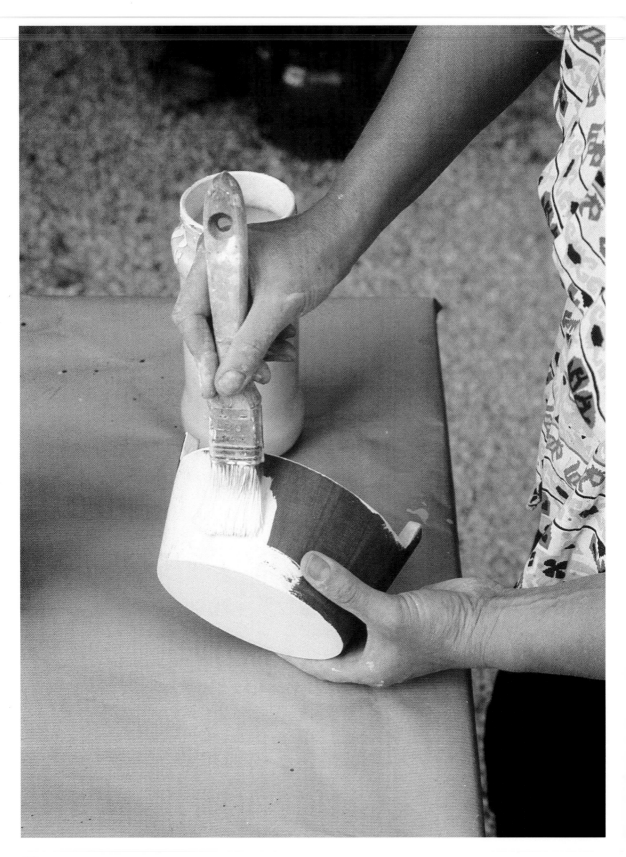

3. Opposite page: *Carefully apply an*
even coat of the background colour, then
let dry for 12 hours.

4. *Rub the paintwork back with*
a wet scotchbrite.

The background is finished and the tubs
are ready to be decorated.

5. Draw the design on to the tub in white chalk – using tracing paper on a curved surface can be difficult.

7. Opposite, top: *Once the motif is thoroughly dry, apply three coats of satin-finish acrylic varnish.*

8. Opposite, bottom: *The final step: adding the patina, a mixture of Judean bitumen and turpentine.*

6. Painting the motif: first the leaves (above), *then the fruit* (right).

A CORNER CUPBOARD

The palette:

The corner cupboard in its original state.

Working step by step

1. Tint the wood to the tone you want with walnut stain. Let dry for 12 hours.

2. Coat the entire surface with a matt acrylic varnish, let dry for 12 hours, then rub down with fine sandpaper.

3. Give the piece a coat of white paint. You can use pure, untinted white here: when you put the patina on later you'll get that desirable 'off-white' look. Let dry for 12 hours.

4. Rub the paintwork down with a wet scotchbrite.

5. The drawer and the door panel are going to be decorated. Prepare your designs on tracing paper, then transfer them on to the cupboard.

6. As to the makeup of the motifs, this composition includes grapes (fruit example 11), wheat (example 16) and a basket (model A, page 32). We used only a dark blue and white: to get two lighter shades of blue, it sufficed to add the right amount of white.

Your paint should be ready in advance, in pots.

In this example you should paint the elements of the motif

This piece of furniture is in raw pine – it has not been stained, varnished or waxed.
Once again we're going to use the technique for painting directly on to wood, as outlined on page 13.

The corner cupboard after decoration.

in the following order:
– the leaves;
– the wheat;
– the basket;
– the grapes.

7. Paint the moulding in dark blue. Do the same around the border of the top and down near the base.

8. When the motif has thoroughly dried, you can apply your 3 coats of acrylic varnish.

9. Brush the patina on, then wipe it down as per the instructions on page 15.

59

1. You begin by tinting the wood with walnut stain. Let the stain dry for 12 hours, then add a coat of matt acrylic varnish. Let dry another 12 hours.

2. Left: *Having rubbed the surface down with fine sandpaper, paint the piece with plain white paint and let dry for 12 hours.*

3. Above: *The paint now has to be rubbed back with a wet scotchbrite.*

4. *Prepare your design on sheets of tracing paper, then transfer them on to the areas concerned.*

5. *For the door, we used a flowers and fruit composition.*

6. You begin the motif with the leaves.

7. Then you move on
to the painting of the wheat.

8. After the wheat, it's the turn
of the basket.

9. Last of all, the grapes.

10. The moulding is painted with dark blue.

11. When the entire motif is dry, it's time to cover it with three coats of acrylic varnish.

12. Brushing on the patina: once this has been done, wipe down according to the instructions on page 15.

A CHEST OF DRAWERS

The palette:

Before being decorated, the chest of drawers was new and covered with a coat of varnish.

This chest of drawers came to us already varnished. This posed certain problems, varnish not being an easy substance to strip off. As a result, there was no question of staining the wood and using the same technique as before. In a case like this you fall back on the technique described on page 13: Painting the background on to a beige base-coat.

Working step by step
1. Rub the piece of furniture with a rag soaked in acetone, so as to make the varnish porous. This way you get a better key for your paint.

2. Paint on a coat of beige, let dry for 12 hours.

3. Stick scotch tape around the edges of the drawers to create a false moulding.

4. Paint a single coat of light green on to the drawers and a darker green on to the body of the chest of drawers. Let dry for 12 hours.

5. Strip the scotch tape off the drawers.

6. Rub the paint back with a damp scotchbrite, so as to let the underlying surface show through in places. The exact 'ageing' effect to be obtained will depend on you.

7. When the background paintwork is finished, you can start on your decoration. We opted for a combination of roses (flowers, example 3) and birds (page 34).

8. Draw the motif on tracing paper. If your design is symmetrical, you'll only have to draw one half of it – you'll be able to create the second half by folding the paper over on itself once the first half has been transferred.

Quite a change! The same chest of drawers after being decorated.

In all you'll need three different tracings: some of the drawers are identical. When transferring your designs, pay close attention to the order of the drawers; the best idea is to number them clearly before you start.

9. Begin the decoration with the leaves on the drawers.

10. Next step: the roses.

11. Finish with the berries and the birds.

12. It was only when the motif had been finished that we decided on the colour of the 'false moulding'. This decision was based on the decor and on the need to get a good balance. The colour chosen was straw yellow, the same as for the roses.

13. When everything is good and dry, apply your three coats of acrylic varnish.

14. Last of all, apply the patina, as explained on page 15.

1. Above: *Rub the chest of drawers down with acetone, to make the varnish porous. This will give the various coats of paint a better grip.*

2. Right, top: *Apply a coat of beige paint and let it dry for 12 hours.*

3. Right: *A band of scotch tape around the edge of the drawers allows the creation of a false moulding.*

4. A single coat of light green for the drawers and a single coat of dark green for the body of the piece. Let dry for 12 hours.

5. The scotch tape is removed from the drawers.

6. By rubbing back the paint with a damp scotchbrite, we let the beige base-coat show through. It's up to you to choose the degree of 'wear'.

7. With the basic paintwork done, it's time to start the decoration.

8. The motif is laid out on tracing paper. Since it's symmetrical, one half of each motif will suffice: you'll be able to create the second half simply by folding the sheet of tracing paper along its midline.

9. The decoration begins with the foliage on the drawers.

10. We continue with the roses.

11. We finish with the berries and the birds. Once the motif is in place, you can choose a matching colour for the moulding.

12. When the whole piece is dry, it's time to apply three coats of acrylic varnish – without forgetting the drying time (12 hours) between coats.

13. For the patina, follow the procedure explained on page 15.

A DRESSING TABLE

The palette:

This piece of furniture is an antique and we're going to paint it using the 'sponging' technique outlined on page 14.

Working step by step

1. Paint the whole piece with two coats of white.

2. Create a false panel on the table area, using scotch tape. We're also going to introduce a false moulding around the mirror, in the same way.

3. Brush beige paint on to the false panel area.

4. Wipe down the beige area quickly with a sponge.

5. Proceed in the same way with the area of green paint brushed around the beige. The rest of the dressing table is to be painted green in exactly the same way. The drawer and the upper part of the mirror-surround will be beige.

6. Take off the bands of scotch tape.

7. Rub the paint down lightly with a damp scotchbrite. Be careful here: the layer of paint is very thin, so don't rub too hard.

8. When you've 'aged' your piece sufficiently, you can start on the decoration. Draw the

motifs on tracing paper: the main motif for the table area itself and two smaller ones for the drawer and the part above the mirror.

9. Transfer the motifs on to the surfaces. By folding your tracing paper down the middle you'll obtain completely symmetrical designs. Now you can paint in the foliage.

10. Next, paint in the bow.

11. Finish with the roses and the berries.

12. When all the motifs have been painted, you'll have to accentuate the mouldings – which are still white – with pink. Work freehand, using a pointed n° 16 brush.

13. Now you must varnish the entire piece: three coats of a satin-finish acrylic varnish.

14. Last but not least, the patina – see page 15.

What a difference! But it really is the same dressing table as on page 71.

1. First off, two coats of white over the entire surface of the dressing table.

2. Below, left: Defining a false panel with scotch tape. The same method will be used for creating a false moulding around the mirror.

3. Below, right: Brushing on the beige paint.

4. Right: *The beige coat is quickly wiped over with a wet sponge.*

5. Below: *The same procedure is used for the green paint laid down around the beige. The rest of the the dressing table will also be painted green in this way.*

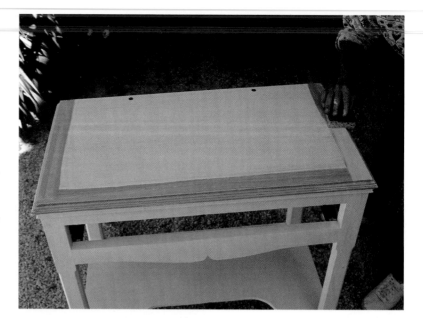

6. *Time to take the scotch tape off!*

7. *A light rubdown for the paint, with a damp scotchbrite.*

8. Now the process of decoration begins. Draw the motifs on tracing paper: the main one for the table-top and two smaller, frieze-type motifs for the drawer and the top of the mirror.

9. Transfer the motifs on to their respective surfaces, then start the painting of the foliage.

10. Next, you can paint the bow.

11. You finish by painting the roses and the berries.

12. When all the motifs are in place, you
have to fill in the mouldings (which are
still white) with pink paint. Work
freehand, with a n° 16 pointed brush.

13. *The whole piece now has to have three coats of satin-finish acrylic varnish.*

14. *Brush on the patina and wipe down with a cloth.*